Sonnets

SONNETS
Subtropical and Existential

JEFFREY JAY NIEHAUS

RESOURCE *Publications* · Eugene, Oregon

SONNETS
Subtropical and Existential

Resource Publications
An Imprint of Wipf and Stock Publishers
199 W. 8th Ave., Suite 3
Eugene, OR 97401

www.wipfandstock.com

ISBN 13: 978-1-4982-6958-2

Manufactured in the U.S.A.

Thoughtful of Judy

CONTENTS

I

WHEN WEIRTON STEEL WAS POWERFUL

When Weirton Steel was powerful and poured
Columns of smoke and fumes into the air
North of Martins Ferry in the valley
And orange water tumbled from its sluices
Into an umber river far below
I was a boy. When I awoke the sky
Industrial gray and close to the hilltops
Was a snug blanket over our house.

Under cover I had boyish dreams
But now the sky is open before dawn
And the Ohio travels sweet and clean.
Our valley is less populous by far
Although I can look backward, take a pen
And populate it with some images.

II

ACT OF COMPOSITION

A mug of Oxo in my hand I sat
Alone in Orpington in a back garden
And wrote about Diana, a pale goddess.

Her solitary splendor over us,
Once observed in Florida in my boyhood,
Moved me to recall her elegance
On a chilly April afternoon
Behind my in-laws' house.

                        How could I know
What part the words I wrote that afternoon
Would ultimately come to play—improved
By two decades of growth—in a long poem
Devoted to someone who was her father
But also bore a low unworthy son?

III

YOU OUGHT TO BE

You ought to be a poet, one could say.

Your memory was formed to evoke
With unusual accuracy days
Of boyhood, adolescence—all those moments
Often forgot by "ordinary" folk—
So now anyone can undo the scroll
And follow word by word your wanderings
And soon become a wanderer, too.

You are one whose Lakes were Florida—
Land of quartz beaches, wooden piers and sea grapes,
Coral reefs and porgies, puffers, squid
And predators who know the ocean ways,
Sharks and barracuda, amberjacks—
A world of truly formed symbols.

IV

BRAHMS QUINTET

One evening in chosen solitude
(Apart from one companion on the sofa,
Our faithful and affectionate young pug
Who loved contact and classical music)
I looked for some encouragement from Brahms,
A clarinet quintet composed by him
Beyond the century mark.

                      The form he chose
Afforded room for all his nature would—
Mature beyond what I could fathom—
Pour into it and make it more than full,
An almost effortless accomplishment,
Perhaps, after long decades of formation
Made him a vessel of enlarged expression
As generous as a constant cruse.

V

WAHNFRIED

"Hier wo mein Wähnen Frieden fand
WAHNFRIED
Sei dieses Haus von mir benannt."
—R. Wagner

Wotan, Fafner, Alberich and Siegfried,
Immortal characters created by
A man who unlike some found no *quietus*,
Who sought to forge a peace by art and labor
Or undo falsehood with a pen anointed
By someone no one ever understood—
One who would transport him farther than
The fall of gods and collapse of Valhalla—

No artist, had he known, can ever be
A god or forge another world for us
Beyond what comes to him from above,
A lofty soul where archetypes abound
And come to us through poets and composers
Who pattern their ideas after them.

VI

SMALL CORALS

A hot summer Sunday afternoon
On a walkway above pale sand
Of Lake Worth beach among a populace
So other—not what I knew as a boy

I snorkeled as I had when I was young
And swam in warm shallows and discovered
Small coral branches in the sand
Undone long ago by Mother Nature.

Corals in one palm I took a place
On a wood bench and overlooked
Atlantic, a concrete pier young once
When I was but now sad and sway–backed

Unlike elegant coral fragments
Or other fair detritus of the sea.

VII

FORM AND IDEA

"Alles Vergängliche ist nur ein Gleichnis"
—Goethe

A power who made us all—who produced me
And who had known us before we were formed—
Made all with forethought and solid ideas
Of what would show as stars and cosmic gas,
Planets and solar systems, asteroids, moons,
And on our modest globe waters and lands
And abundant creatures with singular cells.

He saw them all before they took form.

He also fashioned works for me today
And long ago imagined what they are.

He saw them all before the world was made.

Those ideas are better than my own
Unless I bend my soul to know his mind
Until my work becomes what he foresaw.

VIII

VOYAGE

Should I set forth upon the broad Ohio
On a barge transporting metal scrap or
A motor launch docked by the shore
Of a new river—

                    those brown green waters
Redolent of health and sanity
After decades of *industrious* abuse
By Wheeling Steel and chemical factories—
To what remote harbor should one go?

Ohio Valley was my birthplace

                              yet

Water that composes our Ohio
Was far away from home on my birthday
So I could not call it an old friend.

No doubt—nonetheless—compliantly
It would carry me to the open sea.

IX

WATER SONG

Would you now in whole pentameters
Try to form a way—

              for one could know
A primordial OM and so resolve
Upon a way as effortlessly as
A river flows into an open sea.

Let us embrace One who with no flaw
Or any obstacle that could obtrude
Allows himself to cascade

                  generously down.

Or one could be just a small stream
That gurgles over pebbles on its way,
Home to salamanders and small fishes
Reeds and water plants and muddy pockets
Quite ordinary after all—

            a creek

Voluble with music over stones.

X

WANTING HER

When I was a young, confused man
Who worshipped exemplars of the good—
Monuments of unageing intellect
Yeats had extolled, or in the body a
Young woman of outstanding loveliness
Who strolled along a beach and sang maybe
(She thought no one was there, only a wind
Romans and Hellenes would have called a god
Who tossed her yellow hair in a caress)—

I was fully an acolyte of one
Who offered grace and power for every step
I took along the sand beside the ocean
Or underneath the palm trees at Palm Springs
Or by a brown canal close to our home.

XI

THE CHANGE OF SEASON

A good power engulfed me totally
And turned my soul onto another road.

April and May would blossom, and August
Would carry her large load of summer fruit,
October leaves would swirl in chilly wind
And snow would fall again in Harvard Yard
Before I understood a gradual change
Someone good had brought about in me.
He worked devotedly those days and months
As I walked the streets of Cambridge town
My eyes unseeing on the red brick pavement,
Or on the dogwood blossoms that announced
Winter had died and spring was underway
Now full of hope and unexpected joy.

XII

TEARS CAME—BUT WHY?

Tears came—but why—one sunny afternoon
I took an hour and sat devotedly
Alone with Elgar's *Second Symphony*?

As the *Larghetto* rose up to a swell
Of music that was both happy and sad
Its beauty made me glad but I could tell
It would not last.

           The tones seemed to say
An orchestrator of great music came
And scattered his largess abroad for all,
But at its most exquisite it would pass
And leave us in a silence that was there
Before it came—yet not as though it had
Not come.

          Now its sound world had altered us
And we would know the silence otherwise.

XIII

CRAZY SALAD OR YOUR CHAOS, AMERICAN POETS

If I could toss a salad of sea weed
Or make a banquet of a Man 'o War,
If I could quaff an ocean capped with foam
As though it were a mug of ale or beer,
Then I *would* be hysterically free
And never have to sing as others do
Of broken bottles, dirty alleys, cartons,
Gasoline or harlots, cargo ships
Container ships and rusty chain link fences
Women pining for love or suicidal boys
And call it poetry because it was
American and gritty and "so real."
O morbidly, unalterably obsessed
With who you are you cannot move beyond it.

XIV

AMERICA THE SO-CALLED POEM

"The United States themselves are essentially the greatest poem."
　　—Walt Whitman, *Preface* to *Leaves of Grass* (1855)

America is *not* the greatest poem
Nor are her folks the most poetical
Pace Walt Whitman, who ought to have known
Much better.

　　　　　Afterwards Pound labeled him
A pig-headed father in a pact
And though he thought he broke the new wood
He should have understood if it were so
After a piece or two of useful timber
Splinters would be the ultimate result.

One could put the matter just so:
Our land intoxicated with herself
Cannot produce a word *above* herself—
Myopically misses her demise—
Produces poems that are prose? in disguise.

XV

ALPINE SYMPHONIES

Bruckner at home in Austria surely
Summoned from his nature now and then
Sounds he acquired from a tiny *Dorf*—
A town robustly full on market days

But also full of quiet afternoons
And sunny hours when one could look away
And see something tremendous in the air,
Alpine silences covered with snow.

On open meadows or on forest paths
Remote peaks must have beckoned silently
As he looked upward on his lonely way

And from instruction gathered there in youth
Came forth gargantuan symphonies.

                         They sounded
As though someone had caught the Alps in music.

XVI

THE PORCH

A balm of southern air on Duval Street
One summer afternoon at Key West,
A table on a porch with an old friend
Overlooking Duval and Caroline—

The Porch, an old, two story white house,
Also a bar that sold craft beers
And decked herself with Christmas ornaments
As coconut palms flourished unstopped
All winter in her yard, and southern live oaks
With Spanish moss still hanging in air
Produced a decorous natural barrier
Between the porch and avenues below
Crowded with cars and a trundling Conch Tour Train—

A world evocative of something lost.

XVII

SUNSET AT MALLORY SQUARE

Almost as though a god had summoned them
A crowd in shorts and flip–flops, blouses, T–shirts
And other south Florida attire—
I could recall my boyhood in Palm Springs
When *zoris* were phenomena unknown
To any township north of Jacksonville—
Tourists and "conchs" would amble down to see
Some tumbler or impromptu dancer move
As he or she had practiced or felt moved,
Or watch a small band play close by a restaurant
And offer patrons or us spectators
Melodies from a motley Caribbean

Before we turned and saw old *Helios*
Carry our day beyond Tank Island.

XVIII

IN MUNICH STANDS A *HOFBRÄUHAUS*

"Durst ist schlimmer als Heimweh"
—Inscription on an arch of the *Hofbräuhaus*

A boiled pig's knuckle on a plate,
A pretzel as large as any plate,
A *Maß* of beer—and one after another—
And *Hier*, as Mozart said, *bin ich gern*.

A happy conversation with a couple
On a Bavarian visit from Cologne,
Discreet enjoyment of a band of men
Old enough to have been in the war
Who look askance at young Americans
Who rock a seat in an adjacent booth
And call one *Scheißkopf* just audibly—

Munich in your rebuilt *Hofbräuhaus*
Long after hostile bombs had flattened you
How gladly I would often take my measure.

XIX

CONCH SHELLS

One large conch, old and perforated
By sea worms or sea action of some sort,
Dug gently from the sand in Boynton water.

Another conch fragment, large and fat,
And then another, hardly less fat
At Boston Bay, just up the coast
From a large open pit where black men
Cooked jerk pork over coals and ashes
Of an allspice tree in Jamaica.

As a young man at Lake Worth
I was no prophet and saw no way forward
Unless bound to holy forms of nature—
Bound for good to sun and sand and ocean

And comrade of her former occupants.

XX

DORMANCY

The blizzard of 1950
Covered the slopes above our house and covered
Our 1949 Studebaker
So as I looked across our snowy porch
And down the slope of our front yard
Only a small hump far below
At the top of North Seventh Street
Showed the contour of our car's roof.

A few days later my father shoveled
And made a path onto our patio
At the back.

                After we had played—
And even during play—I could not know
Seven winters would pass and only then
Palm trees and ocean waves would wake me up.

XXI

BALBOA FIG

A wonder of nature—can you remember
When you were younger and maybe more casual
On a mountain path or by a lake?

I strolled in Palm Beach on a paved path
That paralleled the shoreline under shade
Along the Intracoastal Waterway.

South of Flagler's mansion I walked on
And saw a tree with large upraised roots
That looked like folds and snaked along the ground,
So sinuous they almost looked alive.
Someone had called it a Balboa fig
But I was happy not to know its name

And let it stay mysterious, unknown,
So I could stop and stare at it and wonder.

XXII

PUBLIC AND PRIVATE

Almost a holy way, although so public:

A path made for cyclists—and they pedaled
Several miles of dappled sun and shade
Along the Intracoastal Waterway
Flanked by water and those grand estates
Constructed by the wealthy of our land.
Large back gardens sported southern flora—
Monkey puzzle trees, ficus and guavas,
Banyans, and citrus trees in thick profusion—
The many guarantors of privacy
That guarded those estates from any eye
Daring to cast an ordinary glance
Upon those pink and airy palaces—
Upon those stuccoed castles of the south.

XXIII

BRONZE BOLT

One cloudy afternoon the surf was up
And clouded waves washed seaweed up against
Our feet as we ambled among the shallows.

An older wooden pier had tumbled down
Broken up by men who built another—
Concrete pilings, reinforced I-beams
Alien to Florida and strange
To me who loved the wood, water and sand.

We found some broken timbers on the shore
And from one a bronze bolt stuck out
Loose enough to pull out of its socket.

It was almost a part of my own past.

I took it out and offered it to him
And saw it only once before his suicide.

XXIV

A CHOICE

Nor must deformity become a part
Of what we would, or could, or should become:

So many things are real—the ugly ones,
Indifferent ones and truly lovely ones—
And any soul who walks a day or more
Or does not walk at all but only sucks,
Or crawls backward and forward on the floor
Owns a dilemma: opt for loveliness—
And that is not a worn–out option
Although all generations must confront it—
Or "fall to" what deforms as we consume
With all our faculties and then our soul.

Choose a way remote from those archons
Or bold pretenders who command the air.

XXV

PALM BEACH EPISCOPAL CHURCH

Bethesda by the Sea—a stubby tower,
Statues around an old wooden door,
A colonnade with arches to one side
A cloister with a palm tree at the center—
Almost religion enough for one

In our unhampered days of halcyon youth
When blood flowed much like vital sap
Of some fast growing coconut palm tree
On a balmy southern spring day—
Or so I would have thought had I thought
Much about such things.

       His immanence
Could also be compared to palm wine,
Quintessence of warm sap reverently tapped,
Shared ceremoniously by celebrants.

PALM BEACH MOMENT

Come amble along Cocoanut Row
And window shop on Worth Avenue;
Shops and small boutiques abound
For pale tourists colorfully attired
Who wander out for fun. Art galleries
Sport freshly produced canvases
With portraiture and landscapes and much more.
Restaurants such as *Hamburger Heaven*
Or the *Petite Marmite* tempt you and me
And others who may happily afford
A lunch at Palm Beach.

                         Even dogs
Can satisfy their thirst at one small basin
Formed of blue and white ceramic tiles
Located at a storefront on the way.

XXVII

TROPICAL ESCAPE

Among unpopulated tropic isles
How gladly I would sail with a mild gust
At my back to carry me along
And not alone but at my side another
Who understood Caribbean ways

A long romance of Paradise islands

Cast anchor now and swim ashore in water
Much too comfortable for a wetsuit
Or anything of human manufacture
And walk among the shallows and observe
Waves commote the sand around our feet—
Small beige gem stones, a myriad.

Wavelets allow sunshine but also cast
Wavy shadows on the sand below.

XXVIII

COME AWAY

Come away from that long angry shore
And find a way toward the open sea
Or to an island made for no one else
But sandpipers, sea grapes, and you and me
Or any other flora of the sand
Or fauna unpolluted by our kind.

Some would say come fill the cup but we
Make coconuts our cups and such warm juice
Can be our natural intoxicant
So nature is the one who forms our mood
Or we are reformed in her warm embrace.

What matters now is—set foot on the deck
And after all has been thoughtfully thought
Push off

and let the wind commence her work.

XXIX

ELEVATE YOUR WAND

Composed during the andante of Brahms' Third

Elevate your wand as you stand tall
Before an orchestra of any vintage
But preferably old and long established
In someplace dedicated to fine art,
Say, in Berlin or Munich or Vienna.

No matter that bombs battered two of them,
Nor that a hotel desk clerk in Berlin
At your hotel on the *von Bülowstraße*
Had never heard of the renowned conductor
After whom the street was named.

                              So we
Americans pollute all we have touched
That rose above the culture of our crowd.

Now elevate your wand as you stand tall;
Come, bring the past upon us with your music.

XXX

SLEEPY POET MALL

The Sleepy Poet Antiques Mall in Charlotte
Close to Uptown on South Boulevard

Stuff from our wars, German, American,
Bayonets from the Confederacy,
Sepia photos, Nazi medals, coins,
Paintings from Europe by unknown artists—
One a romantic castle overlooking
A valley no one now would recognize—
Old furniture well suited to make
A brace of rooms look more than civilized,
Vintage clothes and vinyl records, sterling
Napkin rings, a faded print of Haydn,
Mozart, Beethoven, Brahms . . .

A mall where one could soon be at home.

XXXI

AFLOAT OFF PALM BEACH

Proper coastal water gave way
To other water, a profounder blue;
Our cabin cruiser had found the Gulf Stream.

We dropped anchor and also cast
Fishing lines—although I had no rod
As I was too young for deep sea fishing.

The Gulf Stream was an ideal place to float
Because of all the fish who called it home:
A multitude who come and go below
And snoop around and look for easy food.

We floated several hours in that spot
And as our boat rocked mildly to and fro
And as the sun shone warmly down on us
I watched the clouds pass by and watched the sea.

XXXII

DIXIE MORNING

A humble cloud, a fog above a field
Full of scrub brush, tall trees far away
Draped with Spanish moss.

                                 Morning sun
Awoke a landscape and also the fog
As we drove through alone on a small road
And all about us luminous beyond
Shadow of canyons at dawn—say
On Broadway, land of luminaries.

Sunrise in Dixie on a spring day

Fog that covers *rosa multiflora*,
Scrub pines, the odd cactus or palmetto,
Tortoises, lizards, rattlers, any errant
Dragonfly or lynx or small mammal—

Us who draw comfort from the fog.

XXXIII

WHEN YOU CAST OFF

When you cast off you would belong
To any shore that once has been
More than what it is today—
Or would you choose a special one,
Sand of an untrammeled coast,
One you saw perhaps?

                    A simple matter—
Conjure up the sand and random shells
And water gently lapping on the shore
Among warm subtropical breezes
A place where you had played more than once
But cannot be now because today
Oblivious of the past

                    hosts an odd crowd—

Nonetheless when you cast off could you
Be on that shore again, haply alone?

XXXIV

COLOGNE CATHEDRAL

As I walked through tall wooden doors
Another world surrounded me—a world
Of lofty and attenuated sunlight
And gothic arches that invited one
To come out of oneself and contemplate
Or journey into a transcendent state,
Not transcendental like the ones produced
By psychedelic drugs and advocated
By Haight–Ashbury gurus, nor the sort
Of meditation practiced by some Hindus,
But a calm and sacred sense—

                              knowledge of One
Whom I could not control, who was among
The soaring arches hammered out of stone
And far above those gothic silences.

XXXV

LURAY CAVERNS

Somewhere in the Shenandoah Valley
Chambers underground beyond our ken
Only men illumine some of them
And show us forms of nature older than
Those who found them—monster pillars, lakes
Graceful folds, cascades and flower gardens—
A place my parents took me long ago,
A haunt of no one in particular,
An architecture of water and stone
Arose as I lay in the sun and sought
An ideal companion to a thought

About tomorrow and a day after.

An outsider has lit our caverns large
But someday he will take away the torch.

XXXVI

HARVARD SQUARE REDUX

Harvard Square on a sunny morning—
Tufts of cloud cast fast moving shadows
On asphalt, low roofs, umbrellas and chairs
Of outdoor cafés as they hurry on.

Once more among them as an outsider
Also one who never was at home
Among the ebb and flow of urban traffic
Or the colonial ambience of Harvard

Down the small stairwell of Raven Used Books
I walk and look around.

                  In other days
I was a student and there was no Raven;
Mostly what they sold was not yet.

At home by the woods our sounds are largely
Harbored by a wind that drives the clouds.

XXXVII

HOW CAN ONE ESCAPE?

If you would escape a somber mood
Or lethargy that captures your soul
Not because the day is cloudy or
You are bored, or have no friend to pass
An hour or two—causes you may find
In younger souls—but because you know
Unsoundness of family circumstances
Or else more broadly the monstrous decay
That gnaws our social fabric 'til it frays
And comes unraveled as it must soon do
As God counts soon—

           Come then and wander down
A path that conducts you to younger days
And know a love affair you had before—

One who has loved can surely

              love once more.

XXXVIII

EL GRECO'S TOLEDO

Remote from putative roots in Byzantium
Or Plato or Plotinus come to us
Elongated portrayals, Mary, Jesus—
Art almost surreal before Dali

And on a hill of almost natural contours
Under a sky almost supernal Toledo
Towers pliable and much like clay.

She can be approached by a road arched
Over a chasm like an aqueduct
And through a passage in a tall turret,
A gate opened or closed at the command
Of a holy one within.

                    O Luminous
More than the sky and clouds you illuminate,
Illumine one leaden soul like them.

XXXIX

CLOUDS

Flat out I lay on our back lawn
On North Seventh Street and saw thin clouds
So far above I felt almost as though
I was about to fall up into them—
A sudden trip upward, disoriented,
Dizzy—and yet I just lay still.

On the other hand in Florida
Cumulus towers puffy white and full
Of power or like scoops of peach ice cream
Afloat serene far to the south of us
As we stood on a shore and saw the ocean
Serenade warm sand as evening fell—

Anyone could watch them gladly
Mutate grandly or float into darkness.

XL

A BOY ASTRONOMER

Once I was a boy astronomer
At Palm Springs, and on January nights—
Clear when air was cool and up above
Stars and planets in a lucid sky
And the Milky Way a band of fog
Hung unperturbed by any gaze—
A part of me longed to be born
Centuries from now when some humans
In saucers—as shown in *Forbidden Planet*—
Wandered through the galaxy.

                  A boy
Would be a star trooper or an explorer
Unaware how hazardous the voyage
How strong the opposition from some quarter

And unaware of a nobler way.

XLI

YERBA BUENA

Yerba Buena Gardens at the core
Of San Francisco, a small patch of green
And a fringe of trees, only a few,
Commemorate a Swiss adventurer,
Sutter, whose mill and growing colony
Augured prosperity and fruitfulness
Unknown before in California—
But as a goddess with her yellow hair
Can make a normal man a fool

                             so gold
Summoned a crowd of fools who would undo
A horn of plenty just about to yield—

O cornucopia of ample harvest.

No rash forty niner at the brook
Understood the flashes in his pan.

XLII

SEA GLASS

Dark blue, green and orange, translucent
On weathered grey wood they sat and from
A fence post looked across a sandy beach
Fringed with sea oats—a coastal view
Almost quintessentially New England
But ocean smoothed their broken edges, dimpled
Their contoured surfaces almost as though
By a spell—Ocean who knows no homeland

And no state can own her magnitude.

From a careless fishing boat or sailboat
Or Boston Whaler they dropped into water
And were transformed by a generous goddess
Who alters all who come into her world

Of whatever hue or composition.

XLIII

DAPHNE AND APOLLO

— On seeing Bernini's sculpture in the Galleria Borghese, Rome

Daphne why flee one who came down
Carnal embodiment as it would seem
Of heavenly radiance, Apollo sun
Of amorous intent, who would love you
As no one else could love?

                  Or why now alter
Your lithe and lovely form, so ingénue
Who had so much to offer to a god
Or any man and turn to loathsome wood—
Awful by comparison although
Wood could be innocent or even useful?

None have a satisfactory answer
Although we stand in awe of what Bernini
Accomplished with a mallet and some marble—
A transformation turned by a master.

XLIV

A SHIP OF FOOLS

Proud from Liverpool she hoisted anchor
Amid fanfare and no small boast
Made by a deck hand, "God himself
Could not sink this ship."

                    Nor alone
Did a menial assume the best
Of molded steel and some three billion bolts
The consummation of a calculation
Made by ones too small to grasp the truth.

How marvelous her cargo—autos, silks
Straw hats, vermouth, an ancient Rubaiyat
Bound with a thousand gem stones and much more,
Valuables consigned to Tiffany
Goods to Spaulding, Brown Brothers and Saks

Accompanied so many to the bottom.

XLV

DOVE COTTAGE

Dove Cottage in the Lakes how crowded now
Your environs hardly so pastoral
As long ago when you were home to one
Who walked your mountains, saw your rivulets
And cumulus clouds hang stationary over
A patchwork county dappled by their shadows.

As a young man I walked your ways
And came to love both Lakes and vistas
Offered by Walla Crag, Skiddaw, Helvellyn
And her parlous ridge—

                                    when not in cloud.

Once on her foggy top I gave a lamb
A ham sandwich and saw the outer crust
Surround her chops as it hung there
Articulate as it were of a smile.

XLVI

SUN AND WOOD

On our playground at Lake Worth Junior High—
Nor playground surely but a battleground
Where a coach had us do calisthenics
One of seven periods, ours the last—

An open park of trees and scrub brush
Afforded us a play area
And we could hide and pick up random wood
And focus solar rays onto one spot
Using a magnifying glass from home.

How the spot would darken, smolder, burn
And tantalize us with a sweet aroma.

A memory almost as sweet I hold
As it comes back to me and I consider
How young I was that day—

           how innocent.

XLVII

CHISLEHURST CAVES

Constructed by the Romans long ago
Or perhaps Druids took a spade in hand
Or Saxons who voyaged from Holstein hopeful
Of goods more useful or valuable
Than what one sees—

               over twenty miles
Of cavern, tortuous and black unless
Somebody cast pale light on the walls.

Circa 1250 records first declare
Them only shafts of those who dug for chalk
And flint.

        A modest unromantic start
For such a work. Surely it offers us
Room for speculation. We conjure
Bygone occult rituals or a tale
Akin to

    The Cask of Amontillado

XLVIII

SAVIOR OF A FISH

A song of Palm Beach Inlet her pump house
And rocky barrier almost found a way
Out of my soul as I lay in the sun

But another memory rose up.

One afternoon at Lake Worth beach
I snorkeled in the sun and saw a snapper
Silver red and gleaming as he swam
Unaware of an impending harm
But I noticed what caught his attention,
Shrimp on a hook and a long nylon line—
Doubtless someone standing on the pier
At the other end.

                I grabbed and pulled
And saw the hook draw rapidly away—

A snapper saved to hunt another day.

XLIX

PANTANAL

A paradise I never imagined,
Far south of Florida the one I loved,
Paraguay Bolivia and Brazil
Are owned by you—or own you, but what man
Could boast you rank among his possessions?

Who can own the hyacinth macaws
Command the capybaras or assume
Authority over the jaguar?
A giant anteater has other matters
In mind and caiman lizards swim about

Without a care for human ambition
As cumulus thunderclouds mushroom in power.

On iron gray foundations they advance
And drop torrential sheets in mid–October.

L

WOULD IT MAKE YOU ANGRY?

Would it make you angry to peruse
Volume after volume of our poems
Or poem after poem if not a volume
Because your anger and frustration
Would stop you after one poem or two?

Are you so much an ideologue
That only one sort of poem can please
Or only one style?

                    Or is it that
No poetry could ever come close
To what a good composer can produce
And so the "music" always falls short
In poem heroic, limerick or sonnet?

Or would you amble with a walking stick
Or put a posy in m' lady's bonnet?

LI

NULL AND MOON

A seminar I took with Harold Bloom
But—far more important—two boys grown
To poetry once they had come of age . . .

One boy did master circus animals
And made Robartes dance and peacocks spread
Gorgeous fans for general bemusement.

One boy through an uncle's monocle,
Persuaded all was null, yet made us poems
And was almost seduced by Key West.

One saw chaos in cosmic abundance;
Across the sea his brother poet forged
Chaos to One under a waning moon.

But later I—with family from above—
Supped under a full moon

south of Stock Island.

LII

TWO GONDOLAS

A gondola sails on a chartered path,
A grand canal or lesser, in a town
Formed for beauty and artistic fame.

A crescent moon also sails above
On a path marked out for her by one
Who knows her and prepared her lonely way.

I would be happy to set foot in one
And sail canals in an Italian town
Or set foot on that other if I could—
But no,

      let me be happy in a boat
Crafted by human hands to carry me
Or anyone who would pay a small fee
Down canals known all over our world
And painted by Turner or Canaletto.

LIII

BETTY ZANE

Chestnut hair flying as she ran
Colonel Zane's sister brought powder
For militiamen at Fort Henry—
Rebels against the King—and gave them hope.

Now they could mow down any foe.
Redcoats and Indians lay in pools of blood
And Fort Henry stood famously.

Of her family tree Zane Grey
Told her story and some frontier tales.

Boys in Martins Ferry saw her statue
In Walnut Grove Cemetery but
As Hallowe'en approached more than one
Wanted to be home

                    before darkness

Came down on us and let her ghost run free.

LIV

GHOSTS AND WOLVES

At Riverview Cemetery above our house
With Johnny Mason or sometimes alone
I walked a turning road among grave stones,
Sat down at the top and had lunch.

Later in bed I wondered if I could
Be bold one night and wander among
Tombstones (although not walk on graves)
But then a ghost or skeleton would come
And scare me—or much worse—

                              could I run then?

Grandfather warned me often about wolves
On the same hill so I should stay away.
Four large wolves with hungry grins
Once advanced on me

                    only in a dream.

For one boy wolves and ghosts were

                              ineluctable.

LV

THUNDERCLOUDS

A storm cloud accumulates over
Our road in Massachusetts and evokes
A thundercloud I saw in Florida,
One that rose above Lake Osborne
And rumbled dark purple and made waves
As though it would engulf or rapture me.

Today's cloud true to its nature,
Full of power, only comes to warn,
Not to take a man to God or a boy
Away from home.

                On his final bed
Beethoven shook his fist at one such cloud
Or so the story goes.

                No apotheosis.

Only a harbinger of summer rain.

One cloud recalls a Cloud Gatherer.

LVI

BLOCKAGE

A toothache shows a poet how a throb
Of pain makes one so lofty head aware
Of its mortality. Nor have I sat
Like Saint Jerome and pondered a skull—
One antidote to over exuberant flesh
In an indulgent age.

                        How be composed
Or allow an inner dance that flows
As words arise on a goodly swell
To swirl and waltz onto a page
An echo of a bygone elegance
Could be a waltz around an inner hall
One knows is song and not just words.

Is art escape from any ache at all?

And then the fruit

                    is sold at mart.

LVII

A MEMORY

Our charter boat labored against a swell
In Palm Beach Inlet toward the ocean

And on deck two gathered scuba gear
Aluminum tanks, stainless steel knives,
Nylon mesh bags and pressure gauges,
Hoping to dive on a known wreck
From Portugal lost offshore long ago
To an august hurricane—

                    if only our
Captain could locate among choppy waves
An outline on the ocean floor of low
Profile and often covered by sand.

Ours was a modest, unobtrusive probe
Down toward almost forgotten wood.

LVIII

ONE MATTER

Work is a matter of a call and not
Only a choice, or would you choose
Just what you want and be American
Down to the core—a son or daughter
Of a misguided revolution?

So revolution has become their blood
And neophilia their malady

Who only know to cast off a yoke—
Or only think they do—and once they have
Only set about to form another
Out of the day's vicissitudes, the ads
The entertainment industry, the news.

But cast off acrimony as

                        the flood
Flows always to an open–handed sea.

LIX

ON A WAVE

On a sabbatical and obligated
To write a biblical theology
I lay under the sun in late July
And thought about another course of action.

I could not catch a wave off Lake Worth beach
Or hoist a sail and snatch a breeze to sally
Far off and away—say, to the Caribbean
And capture fish with a slender spear
Or drink from coconuts washed up on some
Unpopulated shore, haply alone.

Another wave would have to transport me
Just as far but only *as it were* . . .

Under imagined portals in the Keys
One saw astoundingly large southern stars.

LX

ANOTHER MATTER

A young boy I caught a salamander
In a cold rivulet, on a low hill
In our home town.

     Boys back then
Had toy cars and such or played baseball
Or played at soldier after World War Two
Or could do marbles in our schoolyard
Or use the playground sliding board or swing,
Collect coins or stamps and watch TV
On three major networks—or could hark
As *Sergeant Preston of the Yukon* brought
Canada justice on the radio.

Whitewall tires were just all the rage
Elvis Presley was not yet known

And none of us saw far down our road.

LXI

FLOW

One who is just a boy can only know
An age appropriate cornucopia.

His thoughts are beatifically focused
On a small, simple world; he can imagine
Not much, but far more purely than an elder

Not because he has come down from heaven
Trailing clouds of glory as he came
But because he only is a youth
Whose mind has not been touched by our corruption
Or not so much. But give him days among us
Of money, comrades, digitalia
Detritus of a thousand thousand souls
Who lost their way before he came along
And usually he will join the throng.

LXII

NORTH ATLANTIC MOOD

I ought to go to Pigeon Cove or Rockport
Or at any rate someplace close to
Atlantic with her constant serenade
Or since it is New England call her *him*,
Atlantic with his realistic song,
Cold waves that slowly wear the rocks away,
Rocks of a generally resistant coast.

I could not in such waters float
On a rubber raft in just a bathing suit
And feel luxurious—it would be work
Because the water challenges all comfort—
Only the hardy ones would be at home
Or say they were.

           How to end such a poem
When one is not at home

                  when one's at home?

LXIII

GOLD CROWN

After an ache that took away the joy
Of open beauty in a countryside
Washed by showers and brilliant in the sun

And in the office of a dental surgeon
I waited for extraction of a tooth.
A local anesthetic would provide
Suppression of all pain or almost all
And well instructed hands would ply a trade
One would avoid but also clamor for
When there was need. And after the extraction
A molar crowned with gold, washed off and packaged
In one small envelope came home with me.

The gold would last beyond all human dust.
The molar was a precursor of more.

LXIV

BE SURE

Should I be sententious and tell others
Who would aspire to poetry: be sure
Of any calling or election
You feel or felt when you were only young?

A call to clarity today should be
A clarion call, as far as possible
Beyond all doubt, or so it seems to me.

Proliferation of writers and poems
Could be a sign of health or could just be
A sign of cells erupting in a corpus
Itself out of control, and so a cancer
Within a cancer, to be figurative.

A call to clarity is a call upward
For Milton, Cowper, Wordsworth

or yourself.

LXV

WHOLE SHELLS

As though somebody walked along a shore
On a brilliant afternoon—the sun halfway
To a remote horizon—and could pluck
Scotch bonnets and cowries from the sand,
A large variety of shells undamaged
Because no one had ambled there . . .

Call it a figure for a poet who
Wanders along a shore unpopulated
Because the tourist trade has gone away
Attracted by a various mélange
Of shell fragments on sand long trodden down
By young and old who come and go—

                                    whose custom
Has grown so far removed from solitude

Shell fragments tell them the whole story.

LXVI

PURSUIT AND PROPERTY

Can your imagination stand for *aught*
When you are worn down by whatever comes
Your way in a tumultuous landscape—
O fabulous Paradise, land of the free?

Imagination longs for her own country,
Her property, not pursuit of happiness
But happiness obtained, not made by her
But by the one who called her to obtain it.

How could a Lockean not understand
Pursuit of happiness leads to disaster
Not for the one maybe but for the race

Whereas a property calls one to build
A nobler house for sons and daughters
Who could afford to manage with decorum?

LXVII

PURSUIT AND REGRESS

Totem poles, white rabbits, pipes, syringes,
Transsexual or sexual overtures—
Whatever form you are allowed, to take
Young and old without foundations
To metamorphoses of hope, to every
Impossible flagrancy of desire—
Hopeless detritus of our dissolution
You are, and after you are swept away
And those who loved you well and whom you loved
Are dust again—by then another day
Will look upon our history and marvel
At our mature capacity to squander
What came upon us in our adolescence,
A cornucopia that seemed a birthright.

LXVIII

STARS COMPARATIVELY

Stars alone were cause enough to go
Encamp on Key West or not far away
No matter what the hot wind in July
Before we thought of air conditioning.

How would you endure hot sweaty hours
Day or night, unable to doze off
No matter how your body ached for sleep?

Hot air and warm water a rhapsody
Maybe but far more on a moonless night
To stare up at those stars magnanimous
And multitudinous

                and all so large
One's jaw must drop and lungs pause

Now in Massachusetts starry nights
Just offer pinpoints in a cold heaven.

LXIX

AN OLD ALLURE

Some existential core matter was it
Of tropical escape, allure of palms
And coconuts bunched up just out of reach—
And all salvation out of hand
Assured by breezes over the Canaries
Or Honolulu or the Cayman Islands—
And for such Melville and Crane and Stevens
And from England Frederick Delius
Sought somehow a joy ineffable
Just above or below the equator?

A longer also, I would ask of you
What makes a poet want to sprawl alone
Drunk with joy under a red hibiscus
With a hand of Florida bananas?

LXX

ANOTHER ALLURE

Shelly, Byron, Wordsworth, poets all
Advocated solitude and stood
Alone in company, and although they
Advocated freedom as a nurse
To nobler manhood saw in its decay
A precursor of tombstones in its day.

Away all social commentary.

                  Now
A man of that rare calling, stand alone
Among or out of company you must
And only free to go as a wind
Not made by you or anyone transports
To palms to bays to harbors or to sands
Trodden or not.

              Freedom is only found
Once self determination is forgot.

LXXI

A SORT OF FLOWER

A young man who taught at Brandon Hall
Sons and daughters of the well to do
Latin, German, English grammar too,

A solitary room I called my own
After tutorials I sat alone
And worked a Florida poem into shape,
One I composed in study hall that day
As students bowed over homework.

Redone until those images returned
A semblance of the glory they portray
The poem sat alone for many years
Almost as though a holy isolation
Proved ground for other poems to come

Flowers of a long developed soul.

LXXII

WOULD YOU DANCE?

Once more would you dance an inner dance
No one can dance with you, but you alone
A waltz around a vacant ballroom floor,
Vacant apart from images and music
Half formed, half heard or half articulated
Until they bubble up solicited
By one perhaps who made the music sound
And images give substance to a thought
And so the dance becomes a public matter?

No swirl of belle with elegant coiffeur
And gown or beau in dapperest attire
Produces such an air of *bonhomie*
Or exaltation as the one within,
A solitary dance for you or me.

ARRONDISSEMENTS OF THE SEA

Boynton Inlet, Cape Canaveral
Or any subdivision of the ocean
Would suit me now as I haply become
One of those who gave themselves to song
And also give.

              How could a soul go wrong
Enamored of a circumambient sea—
Goddess who harbors all one could have wanted,
Emblem of one she winsomely embodies?

Why would you transport me anywhere
Unfamiliar with tall arcing palms?

Come take me to a coral reef often
So I can be the song I long to sing
And find unwonted happiness among
Parrotfish and porgies and guitarfish.

LXXIV

ALPINE BACH

"States fall, arts fade—but Nature doth not die." — Byron

A lullaby beside a mountain brook
A lullaby of waters almost took
One's thought away from more turgid discourse
About the fall of states and fall of art

And could a landscape of the noble Alps—
Such lofty air—uncloud our thought below
Deflate a swollen anger if one were
Disposed to anger or frustration?

Any other landscape probably
Would do but here a babbling conversation
Of water articulate over stones
Causes no offense and clears the soul
Or clears the mind in any case.

                         So say
What matters more—the water or its song?

LXXV

EXHALATIONS OF THE SEA

Aromatic seaweed washed ashore
Aroma of detritus I embrace
Along with breezes that encompass me
Who stand above the ocean where a few
Before the sun descends at our backs
Face the soft caresses of the sea.

Her curvy loveliness—audacious swells
Have shown me love before

                          and long before
Volumes enamored me of other things
She spoke voluminously love to me.

Donate to me the clarity of thought
To own her beauty yet not be a slave
To her voluptuousness day in day out—

I would engage her as she offers me.

LXXVI

POETA SANS ARROGANCE

"So much alone, so deeply by ourselves,
So far beyond the casual solitudes" — Stevens

A romance, or, better, a marriage
Of one and one where one today, a poet,
May commune with a solitary soul
One's own and be aware how alien
One feels among an educated crowd
Taught in a certain way.

              Only today
Conjure a way away from all the fray
Born of *Angst* who do not know their way
And make an august way to harmony
Of yourself not alone and of no other
But who inhabits you.

             Your soul alone
Is not alone in fact because another
Once entered you and made it a romance.

LXXVII

MUSINGS OF A TWENTYSOMETHING

Sometimes I wonder how it would have been
If I had grown to manhood in a castle
Stuccoed and roofed with red Spanish tiles
That fronted Ocean Boulevard, perhaps,
Or had a back yard bordered by a path
Made for cyclists on the Palm Beach side
Of our Intracoastal Waterway.
Would I have stood in a large, airy room,
And pondered metaphysics, or composed
Music worthy of the grand tradition
I had come to love in Bach and Brahms,
Or written science fiction in my youth,
And later, once I had become mature,
Composed a poem worthy of the name?

LXXVIII

LA BIBLIOTHEK SANS MERCI

Foxed books in a Harvard library
Eissfeld, Barth, Rad, even Bonhoeffer
American tax and tribute paid to them
Of hours and youth who pondered ponderous
Presumably profound Teutonic thoughts.

Today also vassals do come and go
And tax themselves with all they would become
Under tuition of the mortal lords.

But down a road one sultry summer eve
At the stuccoed Busch Reisinger Museum
A long exuberant clamor filled the air—
A steel band in an open square courtyard—
And notwithstanding her most cultured guests

Carried me off to a Sargasso Sea.

LXXIX

PROSPERITY COTTAGE

We lunched at Prosperity Cottage—
So our student called it—

        her back yard
Adorned with cumquat bushes, oleanders
And pink and white hibiscus and tall ficus
Accepted us as though born to the state
As though chameleons or dragonflies
Had wandered into her garden most *loquax*.

Our salad conversation was
Of Harvard, Yale and Palm Beach Atlantic,
Two old, one new, all somewhat alien

And over coffee our discourse was
Of school and classrooms—

        and an ocean where
Unchartered schools in a vast hall
Welcome all who want to study.

LXXX

ENAMORED VISUALLY

How could one comprehend as only a boy

Because all I saw was beautiful
And so engrossing in the palms and breezes
Off the 'Glades or over turquoise shallows

One could not separate love from its object
Emotion from a visual impact
Made by our ocean in her vast allure
Or obviously luscious adolescents
All tan in their bikinis on the shore
Some older and some younger than this boy—
All visually almost hypnotic
In curvy gorgeousness I could not touch.

As a poet and an adolescent
I had come to worship what I saw.

LXXXI

AUTUMNAL THOUGHT

Autumn leaves green, brown and red
On a wet pavement where showers
Brought them down

                 although not petals
On a wet black bough still elegance
Among and through them does articulate
And although I may not take them home
I can recall them almost any day.

On a walk in New England anyone
May enjoy an autumn loveliness
And one should savor it for after all
New England also has to offer us
Hectares of bare branches ashen grey
And stony faces all intransigent
Supplanting aureoles of autumn leaves.

LXXXII

ALMOST I THOUGHT

Almost I thought to throw in the towel
Toss my trowel away—toss all the bricks—

Such as Churchill used to build his wall
One at Chartwell not so trimly made
But about to fall at any moment.

Cain once built a city Horace built
A monument *aere perennius*
And through all ages men have constructed
Architectures of the vanities

So

    why handle mortar block and trowel
Unless someone has made you a mason
Or be an urban planner or a poet
Unless someone has given you a *RATIO*
Ordering your labor every day?

LXXXIII

LAOCOÖN AND HIS SONS

Quidquid id est, timeo Danaos et dona ferentes
— Vergil

Laocoön, Antiphantes, Thymbraeus
Two sons bound for culpability
Of a sexually uncontrolled father
Postponed punishment of a wroth god
But not for long.

          You cannot extricate
Arm or torso leg or twisting neck
Captive *caput* from downward progress
As those cold blooded emissaries drag
Capital punishment down to the deep.
So now

        what moral may be told beyond
One we already know but would avoid

Who cannot save ourselves for all we warn
Being also a long undone priesthood
Before the serpent coils start to squeeze?

LXXXIV

AN ASTEROID

At eight o'clock one spring evening
On our front porch I stood alone
A small telescope in my right hand
And focused on an outer space object
Far above the Ohio Valley.

I would be a boy astronomer
I thought and maybe see an asteroid
And as I watched one breathless moment
I was sure I caught one as I saw
A fuzzy ball of yellow dim light
Swim into perspective.

                          As I went
To bed a small truth nagged at my mind
Before I fell asleep I knew in fact
My asteroid was a star out of focus.

LXXXV

SEASONAL

Summer passes and on her way out
Autumn pursues her with wrinkled leaves
And hints of winter in a chiller air.

Summer amused us with beach umbrellas
Or we could barbecue and sit outside
At home and no harm done.

                                    Autumn instructs
Any who would attend as we fold up
Our summer equipage and open up
Our air conditioned windows to the breeze:

Thoughtfully one may consider now
How much wood and of what sort to lay
Aside for warmth and atmosphere to come
Around a fireplace so long dormant—

Eves of roasted chestnuts,

                           mulled wine.

LXXXVI

WINTER EVENING

—after Trakl

As snow falls slowly at your window
And downtown a church bell muffled
Calls one to awareness of the hour
A goodly spread of food on the table
For any who would come.

                            Perhaps a wanderer
Maybe the Wanderer himself, Wotan
Monarch of Valhalla would attend
To sample what a fruitful land may give
For cold storage and welcome repast.

Welcome wanderer human or god
Lay aside what loss or melancholy
You journey to escape or just forget
On a table before a warm fire
A loaf and wine await your company.

LXXXVII

TAMAM SHUD

Omar old tentmaker whose poems tempted
An adolescent truly jejune
Who thought it almost risqué to indulge
Your songs—for you said come and fill the cup
For "lo the bird of time is on the wing"—
How could a teenager in Florida
Back then have understood a Persian man
Or anyone at all?

        And then a movie
Of you transported me into romance
So I found your poems and could fancy
Those final words imparted by a sage—
And when you reach the spot where I made one
Turn down an empty cup—ultimate wisdom.

LXXXVIII

MEMORIAE

Autumn storehouses now gather in
A harvest of old days begun one spring
In an industrial valley of all places
Plus adolescent crops of memories
Among the waving grasses and palm trees
Of West Palm Beach when she was also young
And grain now come to fullness in the head
Ironically in a cold latitude.

A title tucked away but not forgot
Memoriae of Lake Worth Junior High
Before they tore her down—

                       an annual
Of classmates, daily school, teachers, the prom
A title voted on by all of us
Back when Latin was a normal subject.

LXXXIX

A FROG ON OUR PORCH

Back then—at the end of North Congress
Before a brown canal and just before
Southern Boulevard and the airport
An open field especially after rain
And no human architecture around
A large chorus of frogs sounded an army.

One evening outside our living room
A giant croak startled us and took
Attention from a television show
Commanded all our air and hearing space
So I got up an enterprising lad
And walked outside

                    and saw to my amazement
A green tree frog no larger than my thumb
Holding to a roof support pole.

XC

EMIL'S MANGO TREE

Close to Coral Gables and her landmark
Venetian Pool my uncle bought a house
Blessed with a mango tree at the back

As a boy I watched him clamber up
And prune superfluous branches in the sun
One April afternoon.

                  April—my month
And fourteenth year not fortunate or not
Although it was grand to be a boy
In Florida when she was unspoiled

I saw him cut unfruitful branches and
Bermuda lawn grow cluttered far below

Who could know beyond that hour
Emil's lot would after go to seed

And his mango tree produce good fruit?

XCI

MICHELANGELO'S MARBLES

Unfinished marbles an awakening slave
A slave like Atlas a strong bearded slave
A young slave who does not carry the world
On his smooth shoulders

                       tell us what struggles
What latent power or what listlessness
Informs your forms emergent or what dreams
Repose unspoken as one who made you

So long ago departed from you
A cadre incomplete who can tell us
One sought to liberate you from the stone

Who understood your idea reposed
In solid marble before mallet touched
Or hammer tapped or pounded—

                        one formed
To call forth those veritable forms.

XCII

THE FLOOD

—after Ovid

A wroth god grabbed clouds and poured
Angry water out of them fraternally
Ocean struck a trident on the land
And summoned waters from underground

Olive groves and any agriculture
A farmer may have prayed for in vain
Are inundated and farmhouse and town
Any god's temple any aqueduct
Or lofty tower totally submerged

Sea cows float above a road far down
Under

Someone in a boat may catch
A Spanish mackerel among poplar branches
And all around as far as you can see

Ocean with no coast O Paradise.

XCIII

O JOY

—after Schiller

O daughter of Elysium only
On an isle subtropical as in
MARE NOSTRUM would I dare approach
Your altar flame drunk or maybe in
Another state of mind

                Could anyone
Offer other tutelage to us
Than what we saw when joy became an idol
Offenses that became a sheer advance
Over thunder of King Billy bomb–balls?

May I be happy on a Carib island
And have no care to want what cannot be:

Always in a state of exaltation
About to take the road a *Fahrt ins Blaue*
In a—top down—

             power through joy car.

XCIV

UNFINISHED SYMPHONIES

Composers of partial symphonies

Schubert, Bruckner and more than we know

Grace our concert halls or not . . .
But those two Austrians always potent
Among a thoughtful public. Number eight
Articulate of him—almost done—
And could after all be a total work

And number nine also as the *Adagio*
Langsam

        transports one to a mellow moment
Bruckner's *Leb' wohl*

XCV

HARDWARE STORE MOMENT

Back of the store to buy a can of paint
A quart to cover our wooden front steps
Against October wet November sleet
Winter's dump on us

               and as the man
Compared colors and produced (with aid
Of a computer) an appropriate strain
I saw post cards—no, photographs—he stuck
Above the register

            a solo palm
Arose out of pale sand not far away
A blue ocean under cloudless blue
A wooden beach chair half out of the photo
Barely a cloud and no one on the shore

A sort of comfort on an autumn day
As some of us

         prepared for January.

XCVI

AUSTRALIAN NUTS

One nut blown by a southern wind
Cuddlepie only just born would lodge
With Snugglepot and wander long
Under Australian stars—the Southern Cross
Observant over them

                    what destiny
Brought them Banksia men or an old snake
As adversaries?

                How to be a nut
Simple round and fat and float around
On water courses under sun or moon
Have adventures almost beyond story
Save to younglings who would understand
What it was for little Ragged Blossom
To want a baby

                and discover how
A short excursion to Gumnut Town
Could provide one at a Baby Shop.

XCVII

SCOTLAND SUMMER EVE

A Saga bus tour of Scotland when
We were a young couple—summer eve
With shadowy blue skies until eleven
And under that cool light we walked up
A slope among the sheep . . .

                       How cool the air
Bracing and refreshing at that hour
As though a second life had come upon us
So we behaved as we would never do
In Orpington or Oxford or across
The water north of Boston any day.

We cannot now remove so far and now
The summer sky grows dark much sooner
And not so cool the air and our old freedom

A memory one twilight may recall.

XCVIII

AUTUMN SUN

An autumn afternoon and only sun
No cloud to accent or mar the blue
I lay aside a manuscript and choose
Absorption of autumn warmth
On a blue deck chair.

                   Could any sage
Conjure an afternoon peroration
Why summer could not always be

                           or autumn
On her warm days supplant a coming solstice
So his shaggy white beard would not come down
And smother tropical exuberance
Such as one could fancy in the fall?

One called to Massachusetts must abide
And labor under her many airs
Until

XCIX

ODE: ON AN ICE CUBE

So I stood, and planned to make a glass
Of iced tea or ice cold lemonade
On a slow summer afternoon

Surely it was a wonder of our age—
Water transmuted to a solid
To cool a beverage for a sultry day.

How could Pharaoh possibly have sat
Unmoved to see water formed into pools
In a small but symmetrical tray
Put into a large white box and only later
Come forth as small frozen cubes
To cool somebody's afternoon potation?

O frozen form and wonder of the age
One ought to toast you with a cool oblation.

C

SOLITARY PALM

A solitary palm oval island
Sand enough to hold a palm could be
Sand enough to hold a man solo

Ocean all around a remote azure
And closer up a lovely turquoise blue
Shallows almost pastel almost white

Clouds a few almost a cotton tuft
Almost above the island but not yet

No coconut no tropical fruit
Ocean unruffled and blue above
A small coast no footprint
A palm tree born of sun and sand
Solo occupant

        almost as though

A solo occupant made Paradise.

CPSIA information can be obtained
at www.ICGtesting.com
Printed in the USA
BVOW03*0347040117

472491BV00006B/21/P

9 781498 269582